DATE DUE			

BEAT THE DRUM

Independence Day Has Come

Poems for the Fourth of July

selected by Lee Bennett Hopkins

illustrations by Tomie de Paola

Squeak the fife and beat the drum,
Independence Day has come.
Anonymous

WORDSONG
BOYDS MILLS PRESS

Copyright © 1977 by Lee Bennett Hopkins
Illustrations copyright © 1976, 1977 by Tomie de Paola
All rights reserved

Published by Wordsong
Boyds Mills Press, Inc.
A Highlights Company
910 Church Street
Honesdale, Pennsylvania 18431

Publisher Cataloging-in-Publication Data
Main entry under title.
    Beat the drum : Independence Day has come : poems for the Fourth of
July / selected by Lee Bennett Hopkins ; illustrations by Tomie de Paola.
[32]p. : ill. ; cm.
Includes index.
Originally published by Harcourt Brace Jovanovich, New York, in 1977.
Summary: A collection of twenty poems about this famous American holiday.
ISBN 1-878093-60-6
1. Fourth of July—Juvenile poetry. 2. Children's poetry, American.
[1. Fourth of July—Poetry. 2. American poetry.] I. de Paola, Tomie, ill.
II. Title.
811 / .008—dc20   1993
Library of Congress Catalog Card Number: 92-85033

The text of this book is set in 11-point Galliard.
The illustrations are line drawings.
Distributed by St. Martin's Press
Printed in Mexico

10 9 8 7 6 5 4 3 2 1

*This one's for Marilyn E. Marlow,
and Florence Alexander too!*

From
INDEPENDENCE BELL

Quickly at the welcome signal
The old bellman lifts his hand!
Forth he sends the good news, making
Iron music through the land.
How they shouted! What rejoicing!
How the old bell shook the air,
Till the clang of freedom echoed
From the belfries everywhere.

Anonymous

FOURTH OF JULY

Fat torpedoes in bursting jackets,
Firecrackers in scarlet packets.
We'll be up at crack o'day.
Fourth of July—Hurrah!   Hooray!

Rachel Field

FIREWORKS

They
crash and
bang and
burst and
clang and
boom and
blast and
shake and
quake—

No wonder
my ears
are beginning
to ache!

Lee Bennett Hopkins

7

From
LISTEN TO THE PEOPLE: INDEPENDENCE DAY, 1941

This is Independence Day,
Fourth of July, the day we mean to keep,
Whatever happens and whatever falls
Out of a sky grown strange;
This is firecracker days for sunburnt kids,
The day of the parade,
Slambanging down the street.

That's our Fourth of July, through war and peace,
That's our Fourth of July.

Stephen Vincent Benét

PRESENT FOR AMERICA

I'll pick a bright red apple,
Stream it with paper of blue,
Tie it with a snow-white ribbon,
And sing:

      "Happy Birthday to You!"

J. P. Luby

8

JULY

Everett Anderson thinks he'll make
America a birthday cake
only the sugar is almost gone
and payday's not till later on.

Lucille Clifton

FOURTH OF JULY PARADE

Hear the blare of bugles,
Hear the beat of drums,
Hear the sound of marching feet.
Down the street there comes,
　　Playing, marching,
　　Marching, playing,
　　In the sun and shade,
　　All the music,
　　All the color
　　Of the Fourth's parade.

See the buglers blowing,
See the drummers pound,
See the feet go up and down
To the music's sound.
    Playing, marching,
    Marching, playing,
    In the shade and sun,
    All the color,
    All the music
    Says the Fourth's begun.

Anonymous

FOURTH OF JULY

Fourth of July,
    Fourth of July,
That's when the flag
    Goes waving by.

And the crackers crack,
    And the popguns pop,
And the big guns boom
    And never stop.

And we watch parades,
　　　And listen to speeches,
And picnic around
　　　On all the beaches.

And it usually rains,
　　　And it's always hot;
But we all like Fourth
　　　Of July a lot.

Marchette Chute

I'VE GOT A ROCKET

I've got a rocket
In my pocket;
I cannot stop to play.
Away it goes!
I've burnt my toes.
It's Independence Day.

Anonymous

FOURTH OF JULY

Sing a song of rockets,
Sailing up so high,
Roman candles booming
As they hit the sky!

Sing a song of gladness,
Thankful as can be
For the Fourth so glorious
And our flag so free!

Lois Lenski

TO JULY

Here's to July,
Here's to July,
For the bird,
And the bee,
And the butterfly;
For the flowers
That blossom
For feasting the eye;
For skates, balls,
And jump ropes,
For swings that go high;
For rocketry
Fireworks that
Blaze in the sky,
Oh, here's to July!

Anonymous

OUR FLAG

How bright our flag
against the sky
atop its flagpole
straight and high!

How bright the red,
the white, the blue,
with what they stand for
shining through,

More meaningful
as years go by . . .
how bright, how bright,
the flag we fly.

Aileen Fisher

JUST LIKE YOU

The famous men and women
Who helped our country grow
Weren't always great and famous
Those long, long years ago.
George Washington and Betsy Ross,
Ben Franklin, Paul Revere,
All started out as babies
And grew a bit each year.
They started out as children,
Just boys and girls like you
Who worked and played and laughed and sang
And cried a little, too,
And learned their lessons when they could
And said their prayers at night.
They never knew we'd call them great
And keep their memories bright.

They never knew someday they'd be
Famous names in history.

Margaret Hillert

GEORGIE

BETSY

BENNY

PAULIE

PICNICS

Sunshine and wieners and pickles and ham,
   Not enough salt for the eggs,
Marshmallows cooked on the end of a stick,
   Ants crawling over our legs.

Candy and cookies and peanuts and cake,
   Finding the frosting has run,
All of us knowing we've eaten too much—
   Picnics are certainly fun!

Marchette Chute

AFTER THE PICNIC

On the Fourth of July, Billy Blake
Gorged on wieners, and pickles, and cake,
   And, then, in the night
   He called out in fright,
"How the Fourth of July makes me ache!"

Lee Blair

FOURTH OF JULY NIGHT

The little boat at anchor
in black water sat murmuring
to the tall black sky.

. . .

A white sky bomb fizzed on a black line.
A rocket hissed its red signature into the west.
Now a shower of Chinese fire alphabets,
a cry of flower pots broken in flames,
a long curve to a purple spray,
three violet balloons—
Drips of seaweed tangled in gold,
shimmering symbols of mixed numbers,
tremulous arrangements of cream gold folds
of a bride's wedding gown—

. . .

A few sky bombs spoke their pieces,
then velvet dark.

The little boat at anchor
in black water sat murmuring
to the tall black sky.

Carl Sandburg

FOURTH OF JULY

Remember how the fireworks climbed
    the evening sky?
Up and up a golden trail
Till they burst in shining hail,
And the people down below
Clapped their hands and shouted, "Oh!
Didn't that one go up high
In the sky
On the fourth
Of July!"

Red and blue and green stars!
A blinding flash of white!
Golden fountains dripping down
Over all the watching town;
Rockets zoom,
Then comes the BOOM
Of the fireworks in the sky
On the fourth
of July.

Remember?

Rhoda W. Bacmeister

ENCHANTED SKY

Rose over silver,
Silver over blue.
Golden fountains splashed with green,
And darkness showing through.
Bits of colored stardust
That drift and slowly fade.
What a brief enchanted sky
The fireworks have made!

Margaret Hillert

FOURTH OF JULY NIGHT

Pin wheels whirling round
Spit sparks upon the ground,
And rockets shoot up high
And blossom in the sky—
Blue and yellow, green and red
Flowers falling on my head,
And I don't ever have to go
To bed, to bed, to bed!

Dorothy Aldis

GOOD NIGHT

Many ways to spell good night.

Fireworks at a pier on the Fourth of July
    spell it with red wheels and yellow spokes.
They fizz in the air, touch the water and quit.
Rockets make a trajectory of gold-and-blue
    and then go out.

Railroad trains at night spell with a smokestack mushrooming a white
    pillar.

Steamboats turn a curve in the Mississippi crying in a baritone that
    crosses lowland cottonfields to a razorback hill.

It is easy to spell good night.
                Many ways to spell good night.

Carl Sandburg

INDEX